First World War
and Army of Occupation
War Diary
France, Belgium and Germany

60 DIVISION
181 Infantry Brigade
London Regiment
2/24 Battalion
4 October 1915 - 31 December 1915

WO95/3032/8

The Naval & Military Press Ltd
www.nmarchive.com
Published in association with The National Archives

Published by

The Naval & Military Press Ltd

Unit 10 Ridgewood Industrial Park,

Uckfield, East Sussex,

TN22 5QE England

Tel: +44 (0) 1825 749494

www.naval-military-press.com

www.nmarchive.com

This diary has been reprinted in facsimile from the original. Any imperfections are inevitably reproduced and the quality may fall short of modern type and cartographic standards.

© **Crown Copyright**
Images reproduced by permission of The National Archives, London, England, 2015.

Contents

Document type	Place/Title	Date From	Date To
Heading	WO95/3032/8		
Heading	60 Division 181 Brigade 2/24 London Regt (the Queens) 1915 Sep-1915 Dec		
Miscellaneous	2/24th Battalion London Regt. The Queen's		
War Diary		04/10/1915	04/10/1915
War Diary	Broxbourne Herts	13/10/1915	13/10/1915
War Diary	Bishops Stortford	01/11/1915	03/11/1915
War Diary	Braintree Essex	04/11/1915	30/11/1915
Heading	War Diary of 2/24th Battalion London Regiment. The Queen's From-1st December 1915 To-31st December 1915 Volume 2		
War Diary	Braintree	01/12/1915	31/12/1915
Operation(al) Order(s)	Operation Orders No.1 By Lieut. Colonel G. Elliot Pyle, Commanding 2/24th Batt, London Regt. The Queen's	02/12/1916	02/12/1916
Miscellaneous	General Idea		
Miscellaneous	Operation Orders No.1 By Lieut. Colonel G. Elliot Pyle Commanding 2/24th Battalion London Regiment The Queen's	10/12/1915	10/12/1915
Miscellaneous	Reference 1/2nd Ordnance Map		
Miscellaneous	Operation Orders No.1 By Lieut Colonel G. Elliot Pyle Commanding Left Flank Guard	16/12/1915	16/12/1915
Miscellaneous	181st Brigade Exercise 16th. Decr. 1915		
Miscellaneous	Khaki Force Order No.1	16/12/1915	16/12/1915
Miscellaneous	General Idea The 181st Infantry Brigade are bivouaced at Braintree	17/12/1915	17/12/1915
Operation(al) Order(s)	181st Infantry Brigade Order No.1	29/12/1915	29/12/1915
Operation(al) Order(s)	181st Infantry Brigade Order No.2	30/12/1915	30/12/1915
Miscellaneous	General Idea		
Miscellaneous	Ref. 1/2 Ord. Map Sheet No. 30. General Idea		
Operation(al) Order(s)	2/24th Batt. London Regt., The Queen's Order No.1	30/12/1915	30/12/1915

WO 95/3032/8

60 DIVISION

181 BRIGADE

2/24 LONDON REGT (THE QUEENS)

1915 SEP — 1915 DEC

2404

2/24th Battalion London Regt., The Queen's,

181st Infantry Brigade,

60th (London) Division.

Mobilisation Centre:- 73, New Street, Kennington, S.E.

(d) TRAINING:- During the past month, the Battalion under my Command has been engaged daily in Bayonet Fighting, Hand Grenade Throwing, and Trench Digging excepting on those days when Brigade training has taken place. Instruction in Musketry is also receiving a good deal of attention and a very marked improvement in the standard tests is shown.

(e) DISCIPLINE:- Despite the fact that we have a large number of recruits, improvement has been made. A marked difference has been shown since the Battalion moved into Camp.

(h) UNITS FOR IMPERIAL SERVICE:- A draft of 60 N.C.O.'s and men has been sent during the month to the 1/24th Battalion London Regiment, The Queen's, with the Expeditionary Force, France.

RECRUITS:- No recruits have been taken on the strength of this Unit during the Month.

Lieut. Colonel,
Cmmdg. 2/24th Battalion Lon.Regt.,
The Queen's.

2/24 LONDON

Army Form C. 2118.

WAR DIARY
or
INTELLIGENCE SUMMARY.
(Erase heading not required.)

Instructions regarding War Diaries and Intelligence Summaries are contained in F.S. Regs., Part II. and the Staff Manual respectively. Title pages will be prepared in manuscript.

Hour, Date, Place	Summary of Events and Information	Remarks and references to Appendices
4th October 1915.	There is nothing to report.	

[Stamp: 2/24th BN LONDON REGT. (THE QUEEN'S) ORDERLY ROOM No. C 154 Date 4/10/15]

(signature)
Lieut. Colonel
Cmmdg. 2/24th Batt Lon. Regt
The Queen's.

WAR DIARY or INTELLIGENCE SUMMARY.

(Erase heading not required.)

Army Form C. 2118.

Hour, Date, Place	Summary of Events and Information	Remarks and references to Appendices
9 p.m. 13th October 1915 Broxbourne, Herts.	1 Officer and 7 men of this Unit, attached to the No.31 Anti Aircraft Section were in action with Hostile Aircraft and came under Bomb fire, three bombs having been dropped on the Station, all of which exploded. No casualties were sustained.	

WAR DIARY or INTELLIGENCE SUMMARY.

(Erase heading not required.)

Army Form C. 2118.

Hour, Date, Place		Summary of Events and Information	Remarks and references to Appendices
Bishops Stortford	1/11/15.	There is nothing to report.	E.N.S.
"	2/11/15.	" " " "	E.N.S.
"	3/11/15.	" " " "	E.N.S.
Braintree, Essex.	4/11/15.	Hockerill Camp, Bishops Stortford, evacuated, billets occupied at Braintree, Essex.	E.N.S.
"	5/11/15.	There is nothing to report.	E.N.S.
"	6/11/15.	" " " "	E.N.S.
"	7/11/15.	" " " "	E.N.S.
"	8/11/15.	Capt. & Adjt. H.B.Dewsbury assumed Command of Unit during Temporary absence of Commanding Officer.	E.N.S.
"	9/11/15.	There is nothing to report.	E.N.S.
"	10/11/15.	" " " "	E.N.S.
"	11/11/15.	Orders received to collect Japanese Arms, bayonets & scabbards. G.O.C. 60th (London) Division, inspected Billeting Area.	E.N.S.
"	12/11/15.	Brigade Tactical Exercise cancelled.	E.N.S.
"	13/11/15.	Orders received to despatch Japanese Arms, Bayonets & Scabbards.	E.N.S.
"	14/11/15.	There is nothing to report.	E.N.S.
"	15/11/15.	" " " "	E.N.S.
"	16/11/15.	Orders received to reduce establishment of Officers to 23. Action held in abeyance pending further orders from 60th (Lon.) Division.	E.N.S.
"	17/11/15.	.303" Rifles, bayonets, and scabbards received. Japanese Rifles, Bayonets, and scabbards despatched to C.O.O. Weedon. Major H.B. Dewsbury resumed duties of 2nd in Command on return of Commanding Officer.	E.N.S.

Pulsworth
LT. COLONEL COMMANDING,
2/24TH BATTALION LONDON REGIMENT,
(THE QUEEN'S).

WAR DIARY or INTELLIGENCE SUMMARY.

(Erase heading not required.)

Army Form C. 2118.

Hour, Date, Place	Summary of Events and Information	Remarks and references to Appendices
Braintree, Essex 18/11/15		
" 19/11/15.	Tactical exercise to Stisted Hall Park cancelled owing to inclement weather. Ref. Map ½" Ordnance Sheet 30.	E.M.S.
" 20/11/15.	Tactical exercise in outposts cancelled owing to inclement weather.	E.M.S.
" 21/11/15.	There is nothing to report.	E.M.S.
" 22/11/15.	Colonel Davidson-Houston and Central Force Sanitary Officer inspected Battalion billets, messing halls, latrines, etc.,	E.M.S.
" 23/11/15.	There is nothing to report.	E.M.S.
" 24/11/15.	" " " "	E.M.S.
" 25/11/15.	Tactical exercise to STISTED HALL PARK. Ref. Map ½" Ordnance Sh.30.	E.M.S.
" 26/11/15.	Battalion held Outpost Line from point where STREAM crosses road at Fork Roads above "B" in BOCKING exclusive, to the "E" in DOVEWOODS HALL exclusive. Ref. Map ½" Ordnance Sheet 30.	E.M.S.
" 27/11/15.	Limbered waggons were exchanged at 60th (London) Divn. A.S.C., Bishops Stortford, for G.S. Wagons.	E.M.S.
" 28/11/15.	There is nothing to report.	E.M.S.
" 29/11/15.	" " " "	E.M.S.
" 30/11/15.	Establishment reduced by =18 N.C.O.s and men (Home Service) transferred to 108th Provisional Battalion.	E.M.S.

C O N F I D E N T I A L.

WAR DIARY OF

2/24th Battalion London Regiment, The Queen's,

From:- 1st December 1915.

To:- 31st December 1915.

VOLUME 2.

WAR DIARY or INTELLIGENCE SUMMARY

(Erase heading not required.)

Army Form C. 2118

Instructions regarding War Diaries and Intelligence Summaries are contained in F.S. Regs., Part II. and the Staff Manual respectively. Title Pages will be prepared in manuscript.

Place	Date	Hour	Summary of Events and Information	Remarks and references to Appendices
Braintree.	1915. 1/12		Battalion and Company Drill. Inspection by Brigade Commander, 181st Inf.Bde., of Regimental and Company Books.	"A" E.n.g
"	2/12		Brigade Tactical Exercise. Battalion paraded at 9.30 a.m.	E.n.g
"	3/12		Outpost training.	E.n.g
"	4/12		Company training.	E.n.g
"	5/12	a.m. 9.25	Church parade.	E.n.g
"	6/12		Company and Battalion training.	E.n.g
"	7/12		Entrenching.	E.n.g
"	8/12		Entrenching. Copy of Central Force Telegram No.10697 dd. 7/12/15 re strength of Officers and other ranks, received from Brigade H.Q., this was replied to in my No.87 dd. 8/12/15 direct to D.A.G., Central Force, and copy passed to Brigade H.Q.	E.n.g
"	9/12		Brigade Tactical Exercise postponed until 16/12/15. Route March. 2nd Lieut. P.F.Wright, (Intercommunication Officer) accompanied 60th (Lon.) Divisional Cyclist Coy., on Tactical Exercise in Eastern Counties 9/12/15 to 11/12/15 inclusive.	E.n.g
"	10/12		Brigade Tactical Exercise cancelled owing to inclemency of weather. Company Training. Major H.W. Jameson transferred to T.F.Reserve (Infantry), Authority:-	"B" E.n.g L.D.O.291 11/12/15
"	11/12		Company training.	E.n.g
"	12/12	a.m. 9.25	Church parade.	E.n.g
"	13/12		Company and Battalion training. Alarm sounded at 10.30 a.m. Braintree Railway Station protected against (imaginary) enemy attack.	E.n.g

WAR DIARY or INTELLIGENCE SUMMARY

(Erase heading not required.)

Army Form C. 2118

Place	Date	Hour	Summary of Events and Information	Remarks and references to Appendices
Braintree	14/12 1915.		Company training. Third Army Secret letter 3A/256/9 received re Hostile Aircraft, precautions taken.	E.N.S.
"	15/12		Company training.	E.N.S.
"	16/12		Brigade Tactical Exercise postponed from 9/12/15, cancelled. Route march. Route:- BRAINTREE, CHATLEY, CHURCH END, FULLER STREET, FAIRSTED, GREAT TROYS, WHITE NOTLEY, CRESSING, BRAINTREE, Ref. ½" sheet 30.	E.N.S. "C"
"	17/12		Battalion outpost exercise.	E.N.S. "D"
"	18/12		Company training.	E.N.S.
"	19/12	9.25 a.m.	Church parade.	E.N.S.
"	20/12		Company training. 13 Officers transferred 3rd Line Unit to reduce establishment to 25 in accordance with W.O.Letter 9/Inf./2 (T.F.3.) dated 8/11/15.	E.N.S.
"	21/12		General alarm practised, moved off at 9.30 a.m.	E.N.S.
"	22/12		Battalion and Company training. Copy of W.O.Telegram 1992 T.F.2 dated 21/12/15 re strength of Unit trained and untrained, received and replied to through Brigade H.Q.	E.N.S.
"	23/12		Inspection by G.O.C., 60th (London) Division, Major E.S.Bulfin, C.V.O., C.B.	E.N.S.
"	24/12		Company training. Telegraphed direct to "TERRIFOR", "CENTRAFORCE", "THIRD ARMY", and 60th (LONDON) DIVISION re W.O. telegram 1992 T.F.2.dd. 21/12/15, my Ref.No.126.	E.N.S.
"	25/12	10.45 a.m.	Church parade (voluntary)	E.N.S.
"	26/12	9.25	Church parade.	E.N.S.
"	27/12		Company training.	E.N.S.

WAR DIARY or INTELLIGENCE SUMMARY

Army Form C. 2118

(Erase heading not required.)

Place	Date	Hour	Summary of Events and Information	Remarks and references to Appendices
Braintree	1915. 28/12		Route March:- BRAINTREE, CHAPPELL HILL, FOWLERS FARM, ASHES FARM, Battalion and Company Drill and return by same route to billeting area by 1 p.m. Ref. ½" sheet 30. Lieut.Colonel G.Elliot Pyle proceeded to France on a tour of instruction, Major H.B.Dewsbury assumed Command of Unit.	En.E
"	29/12		Major H.B.Dewsbury absent on sick leave, Captain J.A.McAnally assumed Command of Unit. Company training. Brigade Operation Orders for Tactical Exercise 30/12/15 received. Inspection of Company Conduct Books by Lieut. Colonel H.E.P.Nash, The Royal Scots.	En.E"
"	30/12		Brigade Tactical Exercise.	En.E"
"	31/12		Battalion Outpost Exercise.	En."F"

for LT. COLONEL COMMANDING,
2/24th BATTALION LONDON REGIMENT,
(THE QUEEN'S).

Appendix "A"

OPERATION ORDERS NO: 1.

By:-

Lieut. Colonel G.Elliot Pyle, Commanding
2/24th Batt. London Regt., The Queen's.

Reference Map:-
½" Ordnance Map sheet 30.

Rayne, Essex,
2nd Dec.1915.

1. **INFORMATION:-** Trustworthy information has been received that mounted Patrols of the enemy were seen this afternoon at WAKES COLNE MARKS TEY WITHAM. The 181st Infantry Brigade is halted at RAYNE. The 180th Infantry Brigade are at BLACK NOTLEY, and the 179th Infantry Brigade at BOCKING CHURCHSTREET.

2. **OUTPOST LINE:-** The 2/24th Batt. London Regt., will hold a line from the DUNMOW BRAINTREE road at a point South of the "H" in HALL inclusive to the "I" of MILL north of this point on the same contour line. The 180th Infantry Brigade will be on the right and the 179th Infantry Brigade on the left. The Battalion will be in position by 7 a.m.

        "B" Coy:- "B" Coy. from the DUNMOW BRAINTREE road inclusive to the road running through the "H" of HALL exclusive.
    "C" & "D" Cos:- "C" Coy. from the road running through the "H" of HALL inclusive to the "O" of RECTORY inclusive.
        "A" Coy:- "A" Coy. from the "O" of RECTORY exclusive to the "I" of MILL.

3. **POSITION IN CASE OF ATTACK:-** In case of attack, outposts will maintain their positions and will be re-inforced by the main body.

4. **REPORTS:-** Reports will be sent to the supports of "C" Company.

(Sgd) G.Elliot Pyle.
Lieut. Colonel, Cmmdg. 2/24th Batt.
London Regt. The Queen's.

Issued by Cyclist Orderly 9.15 p.m. 2/12/15.

Copy No.1 - O.C. 181st Infantry Bde.
      2 - File.
      3 - O.C. "A" Coy.
      4 - O.C. "B" "
      5 - O.C. "C" Coy.
      6 - O.C. "D" "
      7 - O.C. Machine Gun Section.
      8 - O.C. Transport.
      9 - O.C. Signallers.

GENERAL. 1924.

1. A small raiding force (MLU.) have landed on the coast between ... ION and ...ATION on the 12th, and occupied CONC...SIN. Three strides of the ... force have been pushed forward to protect the junction of railways at ...AING IN.

SPECIAL. 1924 (BROWN.)

1. On the evening of the 2nd December 1924, the O.C. BROWN force receives orders that as another raiding party has landed the previous day at CRAYDON, a unit of one day should be made to await arrival of further re-inforcements.

Appendix "B"

OPERATION ORDERS   NO. 1.

By:-

Lieut. Colonel G. Elliot Pyle
COMMANDING 2/24TH BATTALION LONDON REGIMENT THE
QUEEN'S.

B R A I N T R E E.
10/12/15.

1. The Battalion will take up an outpost from the "E" in DOWNARDS HALL exclusive on the DOCKING-GOSFIELD ROAD, to the point where the River touches the road exclusive.

   ****

2. The 2/23rd Batt:. London Regiment will be on our right, and the 175th Brigade (imaginary) on our left.

   ****

3. "A" Company will occupy the ground from the "E" of DOWNARDS HALL exclusive to the "D" of DOWNARDS HALL exclusive.
   "B" Company will occupy the ground from the "D" of DOWNARDS HALL inclusive to the right angled bend of the path inclusive.
   "C" and "D" Companies will continue the line to the left.

   ****

4. Ammunition:- Pack animals will be unloaded at Company's headquarters and withdraw to a position in rear of the line under cover.
   Battalion S.A.A. Carts will be parked on the "W" of the BOCKING-CHURCHSTREET ROAD.

   ****

5. Dressing Station in rear of "B" Company's supports.

   ****

6. Disposition in case of attack:- In case of attack, outposts will maintain their position and will be re-inforced by the main body.

   ****

7. Reports:- to the rear of "B" Company's supports.

   ****

Lieut. Colonel,
Cmmdg. 2/24th Batt, London Regt.,
The Queen's.

Reference 4" Ordnance Map.

GENERAL IDEA.

An enemy force is advancing from the N.E. on CHELMSFORD. The 60th Division has concentrated during the night of the 9/10th December in and around BRAINTREE, with a view of resisting this advance on the line BOCKING, CHURCH STREET, SUDBURY. Enemy cavalry patrols have been engaged by our cavalry at 6 a.m. on the 10th inst. at SUDBURY.

SPECIAL IDEA.

The 181st Infantry Brigade have been detailed to furnish outposts for the somewhat exhausted remainder of the Division, resting in BRAINTREE. Sections allotted as follows:-

24th Battalion from the BOCKING CHURCH STREET ROAD to L in DOYLANDS HALL on BOCKING GOSFIELD ROAD, exclusive.

23rd Battalion, from L in DOYLANDS HALL ON BOCKING-GOSFIELD ROAD inclusive to point on 200 contour S of L on Lynds Hall.

21st and 22nd Battalions (Imaginary) in reserve in U portion of BOCKING.

Outposts to be in position by 11 a.m. on the 10th inst.

Lt. Colonel Commanding,
2/24th Battalion London Regiment,
(The Queen's).

APPENDIX "C".

Cancelled

OPERATION ORDERS No: 1.

By:- Lieut. Colonel, C.Elliot Pyle,
Commanding LEFT FLANK GUARD.

Bratkees.

Ref:- 1" Ord. 16th December 1915
Sheet No. 30.

1. White hostile troops are reported to be moving southwards through EARLS COLNE. Our main body is halted at BLACKWATER.

Flank guard:-
2/23rd Bn. L.R.
2/24th Bn. L.R.
2/6th Fld. Amb.

2. The flank guard (as per margin) will march to SISTED, and when the advanced guard has ascertained the village is clear of hostile troops, will move Eastwards in small column formation to clear up the situation towards the GOOSEHALL - EARLS COLNE ROAD.

3. The O.C. 2/23rd Bn. Lon.Regt., will find the advanced guard, the O.C., 2/24th Bn. Lon.Regt., the rear guard.

4. The 2/23rd Bn. Lon.Regt., will direct the attack and will march with its rightresting on the "r" of RECTORY and the north of GREAT MONKS WOOD, and its left BOULWOOD FARM - BENTON GREEN.

The 2/24th Bn. Lon.Regt., will prolong the line to the right with its right flank via the Ford south of SISTED and HOBELLS FARM.

5. The O.C. 2/6th Fld. Amb. will make necessary arrangements

6. The train will remain at the cross roads south of SLATEHOUSE FARM until further orders.

7. Reports (on the march to SISTED) the head of the main body. After deployment, to the supports, left company, 2/24th Bn. Lon.Regt.,

Lieut. Colonel,

Issued by cyclist orderly at ...

No.1 copy - File.
2 - Bde. H.Q.
3 - ZZZZBBZ 2/23rd Batt.
4 - OC 2/6th Fld Amb

181ST. BRIGADE EXERCISE   9th. DECR. 1915.

GENERAL IDEA

The Officer Commanding a Khaki Force on the march from DUNMOW to COLCHESTER receives intelligence, on reaching BRAINTREE on the morning of 9th.December that hostile White Troops are moving Southwards through EARLS COLNE.

SPECIAL IDEA   ---   KHAKI FORCE

The Main Body (imaginary) of the Khaki Force continues its march as far as BLACKWATER where it halts, while two battalions of the 181st.Brigade are detached to move through STISTED and MARKSHALL PARK to cover the left flank and clear up the situation towards the COGGESHALL - EARL'S COLNE ROAD.

x
2/23rd.Lon.Reg.
2/24th.Lon.Reg.

KHAKI FORCE   Order No. 1.

BRAINTREE
Reference O.S. ½" No. 30.
9th.December.1915.

1. White hostile troops are reported to be moving Southwards through EARL'S COLNE.

2. The Khaki Force (less the units detailed in para. 3) will advance at 9 a.m. to BLACKWATER where it will halt; covered by the present (imaginary) Advanced Guard, disposed on the front WHITEHALL-BRADWELL facing East. The Starting point and Order of March of the imaginary Main Force omitted but, the 181st. Brigade leads the Column with two Battalions in Advanced Guard (imaginary).

Flank Guard
?
2/23rd. Lon.Reg)181st.
2/24th. Lon.Reg) Bde.
No. 6 Field Amb.

3. The troops detailed in the margin will act as left flank guard, moving via HATCHES FARM (on the BRAINTREE-COGGESHALL Road) and STISTED to the line BURTON'S GREEN - HOVELS FARM (1 mile East of PATTISWICK)
(Special instructions to O.C. Flank Guard)

4. Reports to BLACKWATER.

Issued at   a.m.

Copy No. 1 Filed.   GENERAL STAFF
"   No. 2 Div1.H.Q.   KHAKI FORCE.
"   No. 3 2/23rd. Bn. London Regt.
"   No. 4 2/24th. Bn. London Regt.
"   No. 5 O.C. 2/6th. Field Ambulance.
"   No. 6 A.D.M.S.
    etc.

Copy No. ...

GENERAL IDEA.

The 181st Infantry Brigade are bivouaced at Braintree.

****

OPERATION ORDERS

By:- Lieut. Colonel G.Elliot Pyke,
Commanding 2/24th Batt. London Regt., The Queen's,
Braintree.

Ref.map:- ½"
Sheet No.20.   17th December 1915

1. The Battalion will take up an outpost position from IVE GREEN inclusive to the fork roads west of LANHAM GREEN inclusive.

2. The 2/23rd Batt. (imaginary) will be on our left and the 179th Infantry Brigade (imaginary) on our right.

3. "A" Company will occupy the ground from the "E" of IVE GREEN inclusive to the "A" of ASHES FARM inclusive.
   "B" Company will occupy the ground from the "A" of ASHES FARM exclusive to the isolated building inclusive.
   "C" Company will occupy the ground from the isolated building exclusive to the "L" of LANHAM GREEN inclusive.

4. Ammunition:- Pack animals will be unloaded at Company headquarters, and withdraw to a position in rear of the line under cover.

5. Battalion S.A.A. Carts will be parked at FOWLERS FARM.

6. Disposition in case of attack:- In case of attack, outposts will maintain their position and will be re-inforced by the main body.

7. Reports:- to the rear of "B" Company's supports.

[signature]
Lieut. Colonel,
Cmdg. 2/24th Batt. Lon.Regt:
The Queen's.

Issued by Cyclist Orderly.

Copy No.1 - File.
  "   " 2 - 181st Inf.Bde.
  "   " 3 - O.C. "A" Coy.
  "   " 4 - "   "B" "
  "   " 5 - "   "C" "
  "   " 6 - Signallers.
  "   " 7 - Machine Gunners.
  "   " 8 - Transport.

APPENDIX D

APPENDIX "E"

Copy No.6.

181st. INFANTRY BRIGADE, Order No.1.

BRAINTREE.
29th December 1915.

Reference O.S.½" No.30
& any map of Eastern
Counties.

1. (a) A Grey Invading Force which has landed on the NORFOLK COAST Is moving on LONDON.
   (b) The 60th. (London) Division is ordered to concentrate at HAVERHILL as part of a movement of Home Defence Troops to resist the enemy's advance.

2. The 181st Infantry Brigade (less the 2/22nd Battalion London Regiment), will concentrate at GOSFIELD PARK tomorrow on route to HAVERHILL. Rendezvous Eastern Entrance of the Park.

3. The 2/22nd. Battalion London Regiment, will stand fast at DUNMOW with special orders (imaginary).

4. The 2/21st. Battalion London Regiment, will march at 8.45 a.m. and follow the route COGGESHALL, HOVELS FARM, TUMBLERS GREEN, STISTED RECTORY. BOULEWOODS FARM, ROMAN ROAD.

5. The Troops in BRAINTREE will march at 10 a.m. at which hour the head of the main body will pass the Starting Point.

6. Starting Point, The MILL in BOCKING.

7. Advanced Guard, composition as in margin.

Advanced Guard.
Commander, Major Dicks.
2/23rd Battn.Lond.Regt.
Signal Section R.E.
One Company 2/23rd.
Battn.Lond.Regt.

8. Main body, order of march as in the margin.

Order of March.
Brigade Machine Guns
2/23rd Battn.Lond.Regt.
(less one Company).
2/24th Battn.Lond.Regt.
Echelon B. First Line.
Transport under Command
of Senior Transport
Officer.
No.6. Field Ambulance.
Battn.Trains in order
of march of Units.
181st Brigade Coy.A.S.C.
The trains and the A.S.C.
under command of O.C.,A.S.C.

9. Reports to head of main body.
10. Further orders will be issued at the rendezvous.

(Sgd) J.N.HORLICK. Captain.
Brigade Major.
181st Infantry Brigade.

Issued at   a.m.
Copy No.1 Filed.
  "   No.2 Divl.H.Q.
  "   No.3 2/21st Battn.Lond.Regt.
  "   No.4 2/22nd Battn.Lond.Regt.
  "   No.5 2/23rd Battn.Lond.Regt.
  "   No.6 2/24th Battn.Lond.Regt.
  "   No.7 O.C. 2/6th Field Ambulance.
  "   No.8 181st Coy. A.S.C.
  "   No.9 O.C.Sig.Coy.R.E.

Copy No.3.

181st INFANTRY BRIGADE ORDER NO. 2.

Ref. 1" manoeuvre
Map Sheet 30.
           Rendezvous
           EAST GATE
           GOSFIELD PARK.
           30/12/15.

1. The Brigade will halt for dinners till 2 p.m.

2. Battalions and attached Units will form in mass facing west S.W. of EAST GATE in following order from right to left:-

  Brigade machine guns.
  2/21st Batt. London Regt.,
  2/23rd   "   "   "
  2/24th   "   "   "
  2/5th London Field ambulance.
  181st Brigade Coy. A.S.C.

2nd Echelon 1st Line Transport and Battalion Trains will join their Units and form up in rear of them.

3. Adjutants and Brigade markers will report to Brigade Major at EAST GATE at 11.40 a.m.

        (Sgd) J.W.Horlick, Capt.
        Bde. Major,
        181st Infantry Brigade.

Issued at:-

Copies to:-

No.1 - Filed.
2 - Divn. H.Q.
3 - 2/21st Bn. Lon.Regt.,
4 - 2/22nd " " "
5 - 2/23rd " " "
6 - 2/24th " " "
7 - O.C., 2/5th Field Amb.
8 - 181st Bde. Coy. A.S.C.
9 - O.C., Signal Coy., R.E.

COPY.

GENERAL IDEA.

Ref. O.S. ½" No. 30,
and any map of Eastern
counties.

KHAKI Home Defence Troops are moving northwards to
the line CAMBRIDGE - IPSWICH to resist the advance on
LONDON of a Grey invading force, which has landed on
the Norfolk Coast.

SPECIAL IDEA. - KHAKI FORCE

The 60th (LONDON) DIVISION is ordered to concentrate
at HAVERHILL on the COLCHESTER - CAMBRIDGE Branch
Line of the G.E.Railway.

ref. ½" Ord.map
Sheet No. 30.

GENERAL IDEA.

An enemy force is advancing from the East on COLCHESTER. The 30th (LONDON) DIVISION has concentrated during the night of 30/31st December 1915 in and around BRAINTREE with a view to resisting this advance on the line COGGESHALL - WAKES COLNE. Enemy cavalry patrols have been engaged by our cavalry at 5 a.m. on the 31st December at LEXDEN.

SPECIAL IDEA.

The 181st Infantry Brigade have received orders to furnish outposts for the somewhat exhausted remainder of the Division resting in Braintree. Sections allotted as follows:-

2/22nd Batt. from SLAUGHOUSE FARM to the second "L" in MILL HALL exclusive (imaginary)

2/24th Batt. from the second "L" of the MILL in MILL HALL inclusive to the second "R" in BRAINTREE exclusive.

2/23rd Batt. from the second "R" in BRAINTREE inclusive to the "M" in FOWLERS FARM inclusive (imaginary)

2/21st Batt. (imaginary) in the "B" portion of BRAINTREE.

APPENDIX "F".

Copy No. ...

2/24th Batt. London Regt., The Queen's ORDER No. 1.

Ref. ½" Ord.
Braintree.
Sheet No.30.
30/12/15.

1. The Battalion will take up an outpost from the second "L" of MILL in MILL HALL inclusive to the second "R" in BRAINTREE exclusive.

2. The 2/22nd Batt. (imaginary) will be on our left, and the 2/23rd Batt. (imaginary) on our right.

3. "A" Coy. will occupy the ground from the second "L" of MILL in MILL HALL inclusive to the "J" in JENKINS FARM exclusive.

    "B" Coy. will occupy the ground from the "J" in JENKINS FARM inclusive to the right angled bend in road under "J" in JENKINS FARM inclusive.

    "C" Coy. will occupy the ground from the right angled bend in road under "J" in JENKINS FARM exclusive to the second "R" of BRAINTREE exclusive.

4. Outposts will be in position by 6 a.m.

5. Hour of relief:- Outposts will be relieved at 6 p.m.

6. Ammunition:- Pack animals will be unloaded at Coy. H.Q. and withdraw to a position in rear of the line under cover. Battalion S.A.Carts will be parked under cover in field west of the "J" in JENKINS FARM.

7. Dressing Station:- In rear of "B" Coy.'s supports.

8. Disposition in case of attack:- In case of attack, outposts will maintain their position and will be re-inforced by the main body.

9. Reports:- to the rear of "B" Coy.'s supports.

(Sgd) [signature]

for:-
Lieut. Colonel,
2/24th Batt. London Regiment,
The Queen's.

Issued by Cyclist Orderly at 9.30 pm.

Copy No.1.- File.
2 - 181st Inf.Bde.
3 - O.C. "A" Coy.
4 - " "B" "
5 - " "C" "
6 - " Transport.
7 - Intercommunication Officer.
8 - Medical Officer.